AMERICA'S GREAT POLITICAL FAMILIES

THE BUSHES

BY CARLA MOONEY

CONTENT CONSULTANT
NANCY BECK YOUNG
DEPARTMENT CHAIR AND PROFESSOR
DEPARTMENT OF HISTORY, UNIVERSITY OF HOUSTON

Essential Library

An Imprint of Abdo Publishing | abdopublishing.com

abdopublishing.com

Published by Abdo Publishing, a division of ABDO, PO Box 398166, Minneapolis, Minnesota 55439. Copyright © 2016 by Abdo Consulting Group, Inc. International copyrights reserved in all countries. No part of this book may be reproduced in any form without written permission from the publisher. Essential Library™ is a trademark and logo of Abdo Publishing.

Printed in the United States of America, North Mankato, Minnesota
102015
012016

Cover Photo: Eric Draper/White House/Handout/CNP/Corbis
Interior Photos: Doug Mills/AP Images, 5, 47, 73; Tim Sharp/AP Images, 7; David Goldman/AP Images, 9; Red Line Editorial, 11; Everett Collection/Newscom, 13; Unimedia International/Newscom, 17; Bettmann/Corbis, 21; CNP/ABACAUSA.COM/Newscom, 23; White House/CNP/Newscom, 25, 31; Everett Collection, 27, 61, 91; AP Images, 34, 58; Public Domain, 36; Ed Kolenovsky/AP Images, 39; John Redman/AP Images, 41; US National Archives and Records Administration, 50; Justin Sullivan/Getty Image News/Thinkstock, 53; John Gaps III/AP Images, 55; Corbis, 57; Donna McWilliam/AP Images, 65; Ron Edmonds/AP Images, 67; Brooks Kraft/Corbis, 69; J. Scott Applewhite/AP Images, 76; R. D. Ward/US Department of Defense, 81; Sygma/Corbis, 83; Phillips Academy Andover/Handout/Corbis, 84; Wilfredo Lee/AP Images, 89; Brian Cahn/ZumaPress/Newscom, 93; J. Pat Carter/AP Images, 95; Eric Draper/White House/Handout/CNP/Corbis, 97; Gabriel Chmielewski/College Station Eagle/AP Images, 101

Editor: Mirella Miller
Series Designer: Becky Daum

Library of Congress Control Number: 2015945391
Cataloging-in-Publication Data

Mooney, Carla.
 The Bushes / Carla Mooney.
  p. cm. -- (America's great political families)
Includes bibliographical references and index.
ISBN 978-1-62403-907-2
1. Bush, George, 1924- --Juvenile literature. 2. Bush family--Juvenile literature. 3. Presidents--Family relationships--United States--Biography--Juvenile literature. 4. United States--Politics and government--Juvenile literature. I. Title.
973.928/092--dc23
[B]   2015945391

CONTENTS

CHAPTER 1

ELECTION NIGHT
1994

In 1994, brothers George W. and Jeb Bush shared political aspirations. It was election year, and both men were running for governor of their respective states. In Texas, older brother George W. was challenging the incumbent governor Ann Richards, a Democrat, while Jeb was running for governor of Florida against incumbent Lawton Chiles, also a Democrat. Both George W. and Jeb were well prepared for the challenges and hard work of a political campaign, having witnessed it firsthand with their father, the forty-first president of the United States, George H. W. Bush.

George W. and Jeb are alike in many ways. Both are deeply religious, love sports, and are well-schooled in politics. They share conservative beliefs opposing abortion and supporting gun rights, while taking more

George W., *right*, is more outgoing than his younger brother and enjoys clowning around, while Jeb, *left*, is more serious and reserved.

moderate views in support of immigration and education funding and reform. And, most important, they share a deep respect for their father.

At the same time, the brothers are very different. According to Marvin Bush, their youngest brother, "Jeb is the serious one. We have always thought that he would have a public career," he said. When asked about George W., Marvin replied, "George? George is the family clown." Others outside the family also notice the differences between the two men. "You come away amazed that these two guys could be so different and be brothers," said Jim Towey, a former Florida official who spent Thanksgivings with Jeb's family and worked in the White House during George W.'s presidency. "I love them both. But they're just very different people."[1]

Victory and Defeat

At the early stages of the election when both men were planning their candidacies, many in the Bush family expected Jeb to win in Florida while George W. crashed in defeat in Texas. Jeb was more serious and had been planning his political run for years. Although George W. was smart and savvy, he could be unpredictable at times. His mother, Barbara, told him she thought it was a mistake for him to run for office.

Yet that night, as the election results came in, the family was stunned. George W. pulled off an upset win in Texas over Richards, while Jeb surprisingly was defeated

George W. and US Senate candidate Kay Bailey Hutchison in 1994

in his bid for Florida governor. Celebration for one son was dampened by consolation for the other. George W. remembered his father's reaction that night, saying, "When I called Dad to tell him that I was about to go deliver my victory speech, he told me how happy he was. But I could tell that he was preoccupied with Jeb's defeat. . . . To some, his reaction was surprising. Not to me. It was typical of George Bush to focus on the person who was hurting."[2]

The results that 1994 election night altered the trajectory of the Bush family in politics. A little more than six years later, George W. used his record as Texas governor to propel himself into the White House. Before that night in 1994, the Bush family expected Jeb would be the next heir to the Bush family political legacy. Instead, it was George W.'s time. "As in all things, it's always good to be the winner," said Bush cousin John Ellis. "So they saddled up with ol' George W."[3]

> **"The joy is in Texas, but our hearts are in Florida."[4]**
> —*George H. W. and Barbara Bush, after the 1994 election*

Deep Roots in US Politics

For more than a century, the Bush family has been part of the United States' public and political life. They have worked as capitalists, senators, congressmen, ambassadors, governors, and federal judges, as well as US vice president and president. Over the generations, the Bush family has made thousands of friends and alliances with influential individuals and families. Often these relationships are handed down from generation to generation so younger Bush family members can call on the older generation's friends for advice. This network has been instrumental in the family's political goals, from George H. W. and George W.'s runs for the presidency to future campaigns by Jeb and other family members.

The Bush family's relationships have created a large network of supporters within the Republican Party, which is important for future campaigns, such as Jeb's 2016 campaign.

Many who know the Bushes say family comes first. Growing up in the Bush family, children learn the importance of loyalty and heritage. They are told stories of past family members and are taught to respect their elders and their contributions to the

INAUGURATION PRESENT

On the morning of his inauguration as governor of Texas, George W. received cuff links from his father. George H. W.'s parents gave him the cuff links in 1943 when he earned his navy wings. George H. W. now wanted to pass the cuff links on to George W. on the day he was "getting his wings" and taking the oath of office as Texas governor. In a handwritten note, George H. W. told his son, "You have given us more than we ever could have deserved. You have sacrificed for us. You have given us your unwavering loyalty and devotion. Now it is our turn."[6]

country and their families. Older Bushes make an effort to pass along the heritage and history to younger generations. Bush family patriarch Senator Prescott Bush, the grandfather of George W. and Jeb, brought his grandsons to the Senate gallery to watch, listen, and learn. During George H. W.'s presidency, Prescott made sure his grandchildren shared in their father's experiences. "They are a clan, pure and simple," said Fitzgerald Bemis, a family friend for more than 60 years. "They think like a clan and act like a clan. Loyalty is very important and so is their sense of heritage. Everyone is independent but also part of the whole."[5] These tight family bonds have helped the Bushes become one of the most successful political families in US history.

BUSH FAMILY TREE

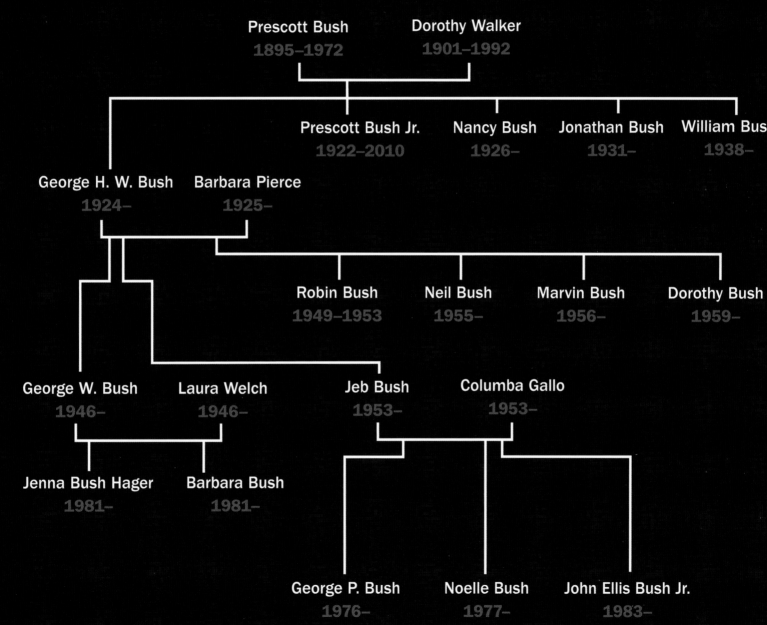

Prescott Bush 1895–1972

Dorothy Walker 1901–1992

Prescott Bush Jr. 1922–2010

Nancy Bush 1926–

Jonathan Bush 1931–

William Bus 1938–

George H. W. Bush 1924–

Barbara Pierce 1925–

Robin Bush 1949–1953

Neil Bush 1955–

Marvin Bush 1956–

Dorothy Bush 1959–

George W. Bush 1946–

Laura Welch 1946–

Jeb Bush 1953–

Columba Gallo 1953–

Jenna Bush Hager 1981–

Barbara Bush 1981–

George P. Bush 1976–

Noelle Bush 1977–

John Ellis Bush Jr. 1983–

CHAPTER 2

POLITICAL BEGINNINGS

Long before George W. and Jeb ran for office in 1994, their grandfather, Prescott S. Bush, enjoyed a successful political career. On May 15, 1895, Prescott was born into the family of an Ohio steel and railroad executive. His father, Samuel Prescott Bush, was the general manager of Buckeye Steel Castings Company, which manufactured railway parts and was run by Frank Rockefeller, brother of US business mogul John D. Rockefeller. After Frank retired in 1908, Samuel took over as president of Buckeye. Early on, Prescott decided he did not want to follow his father's path in steel and manufacturing. He wanted to carve his own path to success.

Prescott served as a Connecticut senator for more than ten years.

SKULL AND BONES SOCIETY

Yale's Skull and Bones society is the one of the United States' oldest secret societies. It was founded by William H. Russell in 1832 and was originally named the Order of the Skull and Bones. The society still exists today, and its members are known as Bonesmen. Each spring on Tap Day, 15 students who are considered leaders in the Yale junior class are asked to join the society. For many years, the society only admitted men, but in 1992, it opened membership to women. Members must swear not to reveal any of the society's secrets to nonmembers. Skull and Bones boasts many famous members, including President William Howard Taft, Secretary of State John Kerry, President George H. W. Bush, President George W. Bush, author and political commentator William F. Buckley, Jr., and Percy Rockefeller, of the famous and wealthy Rockefellers.

In 1913, Prescott entered Yale University, where he studied history, literature, and politics. Outside of class, Prescott was active on campus. Tall and athletic, he participated in several sports, earning varsity letters in baseball, hockey, and golf. He also sang with the school's Whiffenpoof Quartet.

During the spring of his junior year, Prescott was invited to join Yale's exclusive secret society, Skull and Bones. The society was an elite group, with many of its members rising to power in their various professions. Prescott's fellow recruits included Roland Harriman, son of financier E. H. Harriman, and Percy Rockefeller, son of William Rockefeller, the treasurer of Standard Oil. Prescott was the first, but not the last, family member in the Skull and Bones society. In later years, his sons George H. W. and Jonathan, as well as his grandson George W., became members.

Military Service and Civilian Life

On April 6, 1917, the United States entered World War I (1914–1918) alongside the Allied powers, which included France, Russia, and the United Kingdom. As a member of the Connecticut National Guard, Prescott was sent to Fort Sill, Oklahoma, for field artillery training. In June 1918, he shipped out to France with the 158th Field Artillery Brigade. He fought with his battalion on the western front, firing on German positions. On November 11, 1918, Germany formally surrendered. The war was over, and Prescott returned home from Europe.

WORLD WAR I

World War I began in July 1914 in Europe. It was one of the deadliest conflicts in world history. The war was fought between the Allied powers of France, Russia, and the United Kingdom and the Central powers of Germany, Austria-Hungary, the Ottoman Empire, and Bulgaria. At first, the United States remained neutral and did not enter the war. But in 1915, the Germans sunk the *Lusitania*, a British passenger ocean liner with Americans onboard. Then in 1917, the British intercepted a secret telegram from Germany to Mexico, proposing Mexico join Germany against the United States. That was the final straw. The United States entered the war in 1917 and fought alongside the Allies. The additional US troops and resources helped the Allies win the war.

In 1919, Prescott took a job selling hardware in Saint Louis, Missouri. There, he met 18-year-old Dorothy Walker. He was immediately smitten, and they began courting. In 1921, the two were married at Dorothy's family estate in Kennebunkport, Maine. In the early days of their marriage, Prescott worked for several manufacturing companies.

DOROTHY WALKER BUSH

Dorothy Walker Bush was a strong influence on her son, George H. W. She taught him to value modesty and humility and to avoid bragging to others about his accomplishments. She instilled the importance of the team above the individual in George H. W. and her other children. Some people believe these lessons molded George H. W. into a man who was uncomfortable at times being in the political spotlight and calling attention to his achievements, a trait that may have hindered, rather than helped, George H. W.'s political career.

In 1926, Prescott received a job offer from his good Yale friend Roland Harriman. Harriman's family business, banking and brokerage firm W. A. Harriman & Co., was looking to hire new talent. In the years following World War I, the financial houses of New York City, including W. A. Harriman & Co., discovered many business opportunities in Europe. Harriman thought Prescott's manufacturing experience and contacts throughout the Midwest and New England would be a valuable addition to the firm.

Prescott considered the offer. Dorothy's father, George Herbert Walker, also worked for W. A. Harriman & Co. Prescott was concerned that working for the same company as his father-in-law might be a source of conflict between the two men. In the end, however, the opportunity was too good to pass up, and he joined the firm.

Prescott used his new position to jump-start his career and fortune. After the financial crash on Wall Street in 1929, he helped W. A. Harriman & Co. save significant money by slashing expenses and setting up a merger with Brown Brothers, a bank owned by fellow Yale graduates and members of the Skull and Bones society. The two companies merged to become Brown Brothers Harriman, one of the largest investment houses in the United States. Prescott was selected to serve

Prescott and Dorothy lived a comfortable lifestyle thanks to Prescott's job for more than four decades with Brown Brothers Harriman.

as a managing partner of the merged firm. He worked for Brown Brothers Harriman for the next 40 years.

Life at Home

Outside of work, Prescott and Dorothy moved many times during the early years of their marriage. They eventually settled in Greenwich, Connecticut. Over the years, they welcomed five children, including Prescott Jr., George Herbert Walker, Nancy, Jonathan, and William. They raised their children in a deeply religious home and emphasized loyalty and competitiveness. Although Prescott and Dorothy were not extravagant, the family was well-off, and the Bush children grew up attending private schools and spending vacations at the Walker family summer estate in Kennebunkport.

In Greenwich, both Prescott and Dorothy were active in the community. Dorothy spent hours volunteering for

GERMAN COMPLICATIONS

In 1939, Germany invaded Poland. Two days later, England and France declared war on Germany, and World War II (1939–1945) began. Over the next few years, several other countries were drawn into the war, including the United States in 1941.

During the war, the Union Banking Corporation (UBC) facilitated the transfer of gold, oil, steel, and coal around the world. When suspicion arose over UBC's ties to Nazi sympathizers, the US government froze the company's assets. Prescott was one of seven directors of UBC.

a welfare agency and the local Red Cross, while Prescott became involved in local politics. He served as a selectman for Greenwich and worked to limit local taxes as a leader in the Greenwich Taxpayer Association. He also raised money and campaigned for Republican candidates.

> **"We were taught that brotherhood was more important than winning an argument."[1]**
> —*William "Bucky" Bush, on family values*

Call to Public Service

Once he had made his fortune and paid his children's tuition bills, Prescott decided to enter politics. He was a New England Republican, meaning he was a moderate, with liberal leanings on social issues and support for economic policies that would benefit Wall Street. Many of his friends and colleagues had already moved from Wall Street to public service. Now Prescott decided it was his turn. In 1950, he ran for a US Senate seat from Connecticut but was defeated. Two years later, he ran again for the Senate seat in a special election. Dwight D. Eisenhower, the war hero and presidential candidate, appeared on the campaign trail to support Prescott's bid for Senate. This time, Prescott won the election. He served two terms as a Connecticut senator, from 1952 to 1963.

In the Senate, Prescott worked with a broad range of senators in Washington, DC. He sought opportunities to collaborate with both Republicans and Democrats. He

DWIGHT D. EISENHOWER

Prescott strongly supported another Republican of the time, Dwight D. "Ike" Eisenhower. Eisenhower was the thirty-fourth president of the United States, serving from 1953 to 1961. Born in Texas, Eisenhower graduated from West Point in 1915. After the bombing of Pearl Harbor in 1941, Eisenhower held several different commands in World War II. By 1944, he was the supreme commander of troops who invaded France at Normandy. During his presidency, Eisenhower accomplished several milestones, including negotiating a truce to end the Korean War (1950–1953), signing the first US civil rights legislation, and creating the National Aeronautics and Space Administration.

explained his philosophy on the CBS News program *Face the Nation*, saying he tried to take "the best out of the traditional positions of the Democrat and Republican party, and put them together in what the president calls the moderate progressivism of our new Republican party."[2]

Some of Prescott's moderate views included support for civil rights legislation, voter rights, desegregated schools, and increased immigration quotas. In addition, he sponsored legislation to establish an equal employment commission. In financial matters, however, Prescott was firmly conservative. He opposed Medicare when it was first proposed because he feared it would break the budget. He also opposed high taxes, as they would leave people with less money to invest and save.

Prescott opposed government regulation of business and finance and did not support raising the minimum wage because he believed it would cause businesses to lay off workers. At the same time, Prescott generally supported labor unions and their efforts to ensure safe and fair working conditions for employees. He encouraged unions to work together with businesses instead of working against each other.

Prescott's ability to work with people of different political views led President Eisenhower to appoint him as chairman of the Republican Party Platform Committee for the 1956 convention. At the event, the Republican Party would nominate an official candidate for the upcoming presidential election. Prescott was given the task of uniting Republicans around a central platform. The Republican Party was deeply divided over several issues, including the size and role of government and national defense. As a strong civil rights supporter, Prescott worked with other top Republicans to get an endorsement of the US Supreme Court's decision in

Prescott, *left*, speaks with President Eisenhower in 1956.

the *Brown v. Board of Education* case included in the Republican platform. In that decision, the Court had ordered the desegregation of public schools. He succeeded in developing a platform that managed to bring together the different viewpoints within the party.

Although Prescott had never enjoyed being labeled with a title, he asked his grandchildren and other family members to call him Senator to show respect for the office. He tried his best to show his family the business of the Senate and the importance of public service. He took some of his family members to the Capitol building where he worked. His serious nature had a powerful impact on his grandchildren. Lud Ashley, one of George H. W.'s friends from Yale, said, "You can't underestimate the influence Senator Bush had on his grandchildren. . . . The boys had a real reverence for the man."[3]

Retirement

In 1962, 68-year-old Prescott's health was declining, so he decided not to run for reelection in the Senate. After his retirement, he returned to Brown Brothers Harriman as a senior advisory partner. He lived for another ten years, and according to family members, deeply regretted his retirement decision. "He was always bitter about that decision," said his son Prescott Jr. "He was simply miserable after he left the Senate. He was bored and felt that he had made the biggest mistake of his life in leaving."[4]

In 1972, Prescott was diagnosed with lung cancer. He died on October 8 at the age of 77.

Prescott's passion for public service laid the foundation for future generations of the Bush family. He created a blueprint to follow that included education, work experience, and public service.

Prescott passed his passion for politics on to his son George H. W.

CHAPTER 3

GEORGE H. W. BUSH

George H. W. Bush was born in Milton, Massachusetts on June 12, 1924. When George H. W. was still a boy, his parents, Prescott and Dorothy, moved the family to Greenwich. Although the family was wealthy, Prescott and Dorothy stressed to their children the importance of living modestly and giving back to society. They also raised their five children to be a close-knit group and rely on each other. Later in life, George H. W. talked about the importance of family that Prescott and Dorothy instilled in him, saying, "Family is not a neutral word for me. It's a powerful word, full of emotional resonance. I was part of a strong family growing up, and I have been fortunate to have a strong family grow up around me."[1]

George H. W. was a star baseball player during his high school and college years.

In high school, George H. W. attended Phillips Academy Andover, an exclusive boarding school in Massachusetts. At Andover, George H. W. was popular with his classmates, and he was chosen to serve as the captain of the baseball and soccer teams and as senior class president. His sister Nancy later said, "I was terribly popular for a while—everyone wanted to come to our house because they might run into George."[2]

Navy Pilot

While George H. W. was a senior at Andover in 1941, the Japanese bombed Pearl Harbor in Hawaii, and the United States was drawn into World War II. The United States joined the Allies in fighting against the Axis alliance of Germany, Italy, and Japan. Similar to many young men of his generation, George H. W. wanted to serve his country and fight in the war. After his graduation in 1942, George H. W. decided not to go to university right away. Instead, he enlisted in the US Navy. He went to North Carolina for flight training, earning his wings in one year.

As a navy pilot, George H. W. was assigned to the torpedo squadron VT-51 in the Pacific Theater of Operations. George H. W. flew torpedo bombers, military aircraft that dropped aerial torpedoes on enemy shops. He flew 58 combat missions. On September 2, 1944, George H. W. took off on a mission to bomb an enemy radio site. During the mission, the Japanese shot down his plane. George H. W. was forced to bail out of his damaged plane over the Pacific Ocean. Although his two crewmates did not survive, George H. W. was rescued by a US submarine. For his heroism under fire, George H. W. received the Distinguished Flying Cross.

While on leave from the navy in January 1945, George H. W. married Barbara Pierce in Rye, New York. They had met three years earlier at a Christmas dance in Greenwich. In September 1945, George H. W. was honorably discharged from the US Navy.

Life at Home

After being discharged, George H. W. returned home to the United States, and he and Barbara moved to New Haven, Connecticut. He enrolled at Yale University, as his father had before him. At Yale, George H. W. studied economics on an accelerated track, which

In July 1943, George H. W. became the youngest US Navy pilot in history.

FAMILY TRAGEDY

In 1953, Barbara noticed her young daughter, Robin, was not feeling well. After taking her to the doctor, George H. W. and Barbara were devastated to learn Robin had leukemia. In the 1950s, most children did not survive this deadly form of cancer. Robin died seven months later, leaving the Bushes brokenhearted. After Robin's death, George H. W. and Barbara donated her body to medical research, in hope of helping scientists one day find a cure for leukemia. In memory of Robin, George H. W. and Barbara have spent much of their lives raising awareness and millions of dollars for cancer research. In recognition of their efforts, the M. D. Anderson Cancer Center in Houston, Texas, opened the Robin Bush Child and Adolescent Clinic in 2004. For more than 40 years, George H. W. has carried a medallion in his wallet that reads "For the Love of Robin."

allowed him to graduate early from the program. George H. W. was active at Yale, playing baseball and becoming the team captain. He was also invited to become a member of the Skull and Bones society.

While in New Haven, Barbara and George H. W. welcomed their first son, George Walker Bush, in 1946. Over the years, they had five more children: Robin, John Ellis "Jeb," Neil, Marvin, and Dorothy.

After graduating from Yale in 1948, George H. W. moved his family to Midland, Texas. Following his father's example, George H. W. was determined to make his own success and not rely on Prescott's connections. He turned down a job offer at Prescott's company, Brown Brothers Harriman, and instead took a job as a salesperson in the oil industry. In 1950, George H. W. partnered with friend John Overbay to form an oil development company. The company enjoyed moderate success and merged with another company to create Zapata Petroleum. Zapata struck oil in Coke County, Texas, securing the Bush family's finances. In 1954, George H. W. became president of a Zapata subsidiary, which developed offshore drilling equipment. A few years later, George H. W. bought out Zapata Petroleum's interest in the subsidiary and relocated the subsidiary company and his family to Houston, Texas.

Early Political Career

In 1962, after making enough money in the oil industry to secure his family's financial future, George H. W. followed in his father's footsteps and entered the political arena. He became the Republican Party chairman in Harris County, Texas, in 1962. While serving as chairman, George H. W. developed his reputation as a Texas conservative. He always had been good at connecting with people, and this skill helped him build relationships that would benefit his future political career.

In 1964, George H. W. ran for the US Senate against incumbent Senator Ralph Yarborough, a Democrat. George H. W. faced an uphill battle against Yarborough and the strong Democratic Party in Texas, and ultimately he was defeated. In 1966, George H. W. ran for Texas's Seventh District seat for the US House of Representatives. This time, he won the election with more than 50 percent of the vote, and the Bush family headed to Washington, DC.[3] In Congress, George H. W. tried to balance the views of his conservative Texas constituents and his own moderate views. He supported the Vietnam War (1955–1975) and voted for the Civil Rights Act of 1968, which outlawed discrimination in housing. George H. W. earned a seat on the powerful Committee on Ways and Means, rare for a freshman congressperson. After serving two terms in Congress, George H. W. ran for Senate again in 1970 but was defeated by Lloyd Bentsen, a conservative Democrat.

After his unsuccessful Senate campaign, George H. W.'s future in politics was uncertain. Then in December 1970, President Richard Nixon appointed him to a new job, US ambassador to the United Nations (UN). Arguing George H. W. lacked foreign policy experience, some critics opposed his nomination, but he was confirmed by the Senate. George H. W. served as the UN ambassador for three years. In 1973, Nixon asked George H. W. to serve as the chairman of the Republican National Committee (RNC).

George H. W.'s reputation for integrity and honesty aided him at the RNC. He was chair of the party at a particularly difficult time for Republicans. In 1972, Nixon campaign workers had broken into the Democratic Party headquarters and bugged the offices. The crime was discovered in the summer of 1972, but was covered up. Nixon played a role in the cover-up. When the Watergate scandal first erupted,

George H. W. is sworn in as US ambassador to the United Nations on February 26, 1971, in front of his wife, Barbara, and President Nixon.

George H. W. initially supported President Nixon. However, once tape-recorded conversations revealing Nixon's involvement in an attempted cover-up of the break-in were released, George H. W. told the president he no longer had the support of the

WATERGATE

Watergate was a major political scandal that occurred in the 1970s. On June 17, 1972, five men were arrested inside the Democratic National Committee headquarters located at the Watergate office complex in Washington, DC. The men were caught attempting to wiretap phones and steal secret documents. After the break-in was discovered, members of President Nixon's Republican administration tried to cover it up. They raised money for the burglars to keep them from talking about the break-in, tried to stop the Federal Bureau of Investigation (FBI) from investigating, and destroyed evidence. At first, President Nixon denied any knowledge of the burglary and attempted cover-up. Later, it was proved he was involved in trying to cover up the break-in and hinder the investigation. Facing impeachment by the Senate, Nixon resigned from office in August 1974.

Republican Party. At the urging of several key advisers and facing impeachment, President Nixon resigned from office in August 1974.

After Nixon's resignation, Vice President Gerald Ford assumed the presidency. During Ford's administration, George H. W. served in several administrative posts. In 1974, President Ford appointed George H. W. as the US envoy to the People's Republic of China, the chief US diplomat in China. Then in 1975, Ford asked George H. W. to return to the United States and serve as the director of the Central Intelligence Agency (CIA). At the time, the CIA needed a strong leader with integrity to guide and reform the agency. Ford believed George H. W. was the perfect man for the job. In the 1976 presidential election,

Democrat Jimmy Carter defeated Ford. The Bushes left Washington, DC, and returned home to Houston. George H. W. turned his attention to a new goal: the presidency.

The 1980 Campaign

On May 1, 1979, George H. W. announced he would run for the Republican nomination for president. Several other men were running for the Republican nomination, including former actor and governor of California Ronald Reagan, Senator Robert Dole of Kansas, Representative John Anderson of Illinois, Senator Howard Baker of Tennessee, Representative Philip Crane of Illinois, and John Connally, a former Texas governor.

"One of my father's most impressive qualities was his ability to make new friends while keeping old ones. No matter how high he rose in business or politics, George Bush never discarded old friends."[4]

—George W. Bush, on his father's qualities

Although Reagan was considered the frontrunner for the Republican nomination, George H. W. campaigned vigorously. He questioned Reagan's economic plan to lower taxes while increasing military spending. George H. W.'s campaigning helped him win the Iowa caucus, the first major electoral event in the presidential campaign, and established him as a serious contender. However, over the course of the election season, the Reagan campaign switched into high gear, winning the New Hampshire

Reagan and George H. W., along with their wives, wave to the crowd at the 1980 Republican National Convention.

primary, which is the first in a series of primaries held every four years, and going on to win the Republican nomination.

Looking to unify the Republican Party, Reagan selected George H. W. to run as his vice president. While Reagan appealed to conservative Republicans, George H. W.

brought the backing of moderates to the Republican ticket. George H. W. accepted Reagan's offer, although some critics complained he adjusted his moderate views on abortion and the economy to match Reagan's more conservative beliefs. During the 1980 campaign, George H. W. traveled the country, speaking on behalf of the Reagan-Bush ticket and attacking the incumbent President Carter and Vice President Walter Mondale.

On Election Day, Reagan and George H. W. won the election in a landslide. In addition, Republican candidates won the majority in the Senate for the first time since 1954. Americans had voted Republicans into office with a mandate to change the country's path. Republicans believed this mandate was an opportunity to limit government intervention into people's lives, reduce taxes, and return the country to more traditional and conservative social values.

Vice President

As vice president, George H. W.'s responsibilities included serving as the chair for several task forces, including ones on drugs and drug smuggling. He traveled around the country and world, often representing the administration at international meetings and events. Along the way, he continued making contacts that would one day prove useful during his own presidency. In his role as vice president, George H. W. believed he should be a loyal supporter of his president. In some cases, he chose not to express his personal belief on issues, particularly when he differed from Reagan's views. For example, prior to becoming Reagan's vice president, George H. W. supported federal financing of abortion in cases of rape and incest but changed his position to match Reagan's more conservative beliefs.

Reagan and George H. W. easily won their reelection campaign in 1984.

Given his past experience in foreign affairs, George H. W. was frequently involved in foreign policy discussions and decisions. In November 1986, the Iran-Contra scandal erupted. The foreign policy scandal almost destroyed George H. W.'s future political career. The Reagan administration illegally sold weapons to Iran for use in its war against Iraq in exchange for the release of hostages held in Iran. The Reagan administration then used the profits to support anti-communist Contra rebels in Nicaragua. Several officials in the Reagan administration resigned over the scandal, and many wondered for years about George H. W.'s involvement and knowledge of the plan.

IRAN-CONTRA AFFAIR

The Iran-Contra affair began in 1985, when members of President Reagan's administration illegally supplied weapons to Iran, even though the country was considered an enemy of the United States. They sent weapons to Iran in exchange for the release of US hostages being held in Lebanon by Iranian terrorists. In addition, members of the administration took millions of dollars earned from the sale of the weapons and supplied guns and funding to Contra rebels who were fighting a civil war against the Communist government in Nicaragua. The secret scheme violated US law and policy by selling weapons to Iran, paying ransom for hostages, and funding rebels without congressional approval.

Once allegations about the activity emerged, President Reagan appointed a commission and a special federal prosecutor to investigate. Eventually, several members of the Reagan administration were convicted, including national security adviser Admiral John Poindexter and his deputy, Lieutenant Colonel Oliver North. Reagan and George H. W. were never charged with any offense in the matter.

In 1984, Reagan and George H. W. ran for reelection and faced Democrats Mondale and Geraldine Ferraro. Reagan and George H. W. were popular across the country, in part because of the economic prosperity between 1983 and 1984. On election night, Reagan and George H. W. won in a landslide, winning Washington, DC, and every state but Mondale's native Minnesota. They defeated Mondale in the Electoral College by 525 to 13 votes. In the popular vote, Reagan and George H. W. pulled in 54 million votes compared to Mondale and Ferraro's 37 million.[5]

CHAPTER 4

THE WHITE HOUSE

As the second term of the Reagan-Bush administration wound down, George H. W. set his sights on the Oval Office. Because of the two-term limit for presidents, Reagan would not be seeking reelection. On October 13, 1987, George H. W. announced he would again seek the Republican nomination for president. To win the nomination, George H. W. would have to defeat three major opponents in the primary elections—Senator Robert Dole of Kansas, evangelical leader Pat Robertson, and Representative Jack Kemp from New York.

In his campaign, George H. W. highlighted his vast experience in Congress, as the vice president, and in other government positions. He

George H. W., with the support of his family, announces his candidacy for the presidency in Houston.

> "I seek the presidency for a single purpose, a purpose that has motivated millions of Americans across the years and the ocean voyages. I seek the presidency to build a better America. It is that simple—and that big."[2]
>
> *—George H. W. Bush, August 18, 1988*

brought in Reagan's chief of staff, James Baker, and political consultant Lee Atwater to run his campaign.

The campaign did not start off well. George H. W. finished in third place in the Iowa caucus, behind Dole and Robertson. He struggled to overcome an image of being too soft to lead the nation. The week he announced his candidacy, the national magazine *Newsweek* called him weak. But according to Evan Thomas, the Washington Bureau Chief at *Newsweek*, they were too tough on George H. W.:

> *That's an awful word to use, and we used it on the cover of* Newsweek, *I think, to our regret. It was too harsh a word. But there was a perception that he was somehow not a standup guy. He was under Reagan's shadow, and he needed to win over the true right and evangelicals, and to do that, he seemed to be trimming a little bit on abortion, he seemed to possibly be going against his own conscience in order to win votes.*[1]

As the campaign continued, George H. W. grew stronger in the polls and eventually clinched the Republican nomination. After winning, George H. W. searched for the right person to run as his vice president. He selected Dan Quayle, a senator from Indiana. Forty-one-year-old Quayle brought youth and conservative views, which 64-year-old George H. W.'s advisers believed would appeal to Republican conservatives and female voters. Quayle, however, became a controversial choice because critics claimed he was too young and inexperienced to be vice president.

At the Republican convention in August 1988, George H. W. spoke to the delegates. He talked about the improvements in the country during the Reagan-Bush years. And he famously promised not to raise taxes:

I'm the one who won't raise taxes. My opponent now says he'll raise them as a last resort, or a third resort. When a politician talks like that, you know that's one resort he'll be checking into. My opponent won't rule out raising taxes. But I will. The Congress will push me to raise taxes, and I'll say no, and they'll push, and I'll say no, and they'll push again, and I'll say to them, "Read my lips: no new taxes."[3]

In his speeches, George H. W. pledged to build on the improvements he and former president Reagan had made.

In the election, George H. W. and Quayle faced Democratic nominee Massachusetts Governor Michael Dukakis and his running mate Lloyd Bentsen. George H. W. and Quayle promised to continue many of Reagan's policies that were popular with the majority of Americans. They painted Dukakis as being extremely liberal and unable to relate to most Americans. They also accused Dukakis of being soft on crime, pointing out he allowed Massachusetts prisoners serving life sentences to have weekend furloughs out of prison.

In the November 1988 election, Americans threw their support behind George H. W. and Quayle. George H. W. won the election with 53 percent of the popular vote and 426 Electoral College votes.[4] He became the first sitting vice president since Martin Van Buren in 1836 to be elected president.

The Forty-First President

George H. W. was sworn in as president on January 20, 1989. Supporters expected him to govern according to conservative principles, as he was Reagan's successor. Yet George H. W. held many more moderate views. According to presidential historian Richard Norton Smith, this was a challenge for George H. W.:

> *He was looking over one shoulder and seeing where the Republican Party was going. And over the other shoulder, he saw his own lineage, his own tradition. He saw his father, Prescott Bush. He saw Dwight Eisenhower. And he saw Richard Nixon and Gerald Ford, who in retrospect are seen as moderate conservatives.[5]*

Once in office, George H. W. began distancing himself from Reagan. He dismissed many of Reagan's appointees and brought in several old friends to fill out his administration. He appointed James Baker as secretary of state and Lee Atwater as the chairman of the RNC. He hired John Sununu, former governor of New Hampshire, as chief of staff and Brent Scowcroft as his national security adviser. He chose Dick Cheney to serve as defense secretary.

Tackling the Federal Budget

When George H. W. took office in 1989, the federal debt totaled $2.8 trillion.[6] With this amount of debt, the federal government simply did not have enough money to pay for any new large programs. Instead, George H. W. focused on a limited domestic agenda, one that featured volunteerism, education, and antidrug programs. For many Americans, this plan was fine. They had not voted

LITERACY CHAMPION

First Lady Barbara Bush has long been a champion of literacy. Her interest in literacy began with her son Neil's struggle with dyslexia. She believed the more people who could read and write, the better their lives could be. Over the years, Barbara has visited literacy programs, schools, and libraries. She has called attention to the importance of parents reading to their children and teaching their kids to read.

In 1989, Barbara formed the Barbara Bush Foundation for Family Literacy. The organization funds programs that teach parents in low-income families to read and pass the love of reading on to their children. As of 2014, the organization funds 1,500 literacy programs across the country.[7]

SAVINGS AND LOAN BAILOUT

When George H. W. took office, the savings and loans industry was in trouble. Savings and loans banks are financial institutions that specialize in savings deposits and making mortgages and other loans. In the 1980s, the real estate market had collapsed and hundreds of savings and loans banks were on the verge of going out of business. People who had deposits in those banks faced losing their money. In 1989, George H. W. proposed a plan to provide government funding to help the savings and loans industry. He knew the plan would be expensive and unpopular, but he also believed it was the right thing to do to help people who were going to lose their money. George H. W. negotiated with Congress, and the resulting plan ended up costing taxpayers more than $100 billion.[8] The government bailout added to the financial difficulties George H. W. faced during his presidency.

for George H. W. because he would make sweeping changes but rather supported his promises to maintain the course set by Reagan. Despite funding challenges, George H. W. signed two significant pieces of domestic legislation during his presidency. The Americans with Disabilities Act of 1990 outlawed discrimination based on disability in employment, public accommodations, and transportation. Also signed in 1990, the Clean Air Act Amendments put in place regulations to reduce pollution and improve air quality. Yet the lack of money posed a problem for George H. W. He had famously promised during his presidential campaign he would not raise taxes. But he found himself unable to balance the federal budget and reduce the deficit. In addition, during his presidency, Democrats controlled Congress.

While many Republicans wanted to reduce the budget deficit by cutting government spending, Democrats believed raising taxes on the wealthiest Americans was the better approach.

While negotiating the 1991 federal budget, George H. W. compromised with Congress. In June 1990, he issued a written statement telling Americans he may be forced to raise taxes in order to reduce the deficit. The eventual budget included both reductions in government spending and an increase in taxes. Many conservative Republicans, however, felt George H. W. had betrayed his campaign pledge not to raise taxes.

Foreign Policy

During his presidency, George H. W. spent much of his time on foreign affairs, matters that dealt with relationships between the United States and

AMERICANS WITH DISABILITIES ACT

The Americans with Disabilities Act of 1990 outlawed discrimination based on disability in employment, public accommodations, and transportation. The act guaranteed places of business and public venues would provide access for disabled persons to enter their sites. It expanded disabled access on public transportation and provided more equal access to telecommunications. George H. W. believed the act was necessary to allow people with disabilities to live more independently. Although the act's critics complained it was too expensive and it allowed the government to meddle in private affairs, many people believe it is one of the major domestic achievements of George H. W.'s presidency.

CLEAN AIR ACT

Some people believe the Clean Air Act Amendments of 1990 were the most important achievement of George H. W.'s administration. The amendments placed limits on urban air pollution, toxic air emissions, and acid rain. Critics argued the act was too expensive and would harm an already weak economy. George H. W. refused to back down and insisted that by working with the business community, both the environment and the economy would improve. After Congress passed the bill by a wide margin, George H. W. signed it into law in November 1990.

other countries. He approached foreign affairs with his typical conservative and pragmatic attitude. Rather than rushing actions or policy changes, George H. W. took time to consider the options. His past experiences at the UN, in China, with the CIA, and as vice president gave him significant experience in foreign affairs. He also made use of the many international contacts he had made over the years.

In the years before George H. W.'s presidency, the Cold War with the Soviet Union dominated international affairs. Beginning after World War II, the Cold War was not an actual battle but a clash in political beliefs, pitting the capitalism of the United States against communism in the Soviet Union. The clash caused tension between the two nations as they struggled to assert their dominance and spread their beliefs in the world. Because both nations possessed nuclear weapons, many people feared the tension would escalate into a global nuclear war.

However, when George H. W. took office in 1989, relations with the Soviet Union were changing. Communism was losing its hold in Eastern Europe. In November 1989, East Germany opened its borders, and the Germans tore down the Berlin Wall. It was a symbolic moment that signified the end of communism in Eastern Europe. The Cold War was ending, and many people wondered what this meant for international relations. When asked about the collapse of the Berlin Wall, George H. W. had a very muted and restrained response. He said he was pleased. While critics questioned his lack of emotion, others believe by refusing to declare victory, he preserved future negotiations with the Soviet Union. At home, conservative

George H. W. reviews the Soviet honor guard during a Soviet Union visit in 1989.

critics argued George H. W. should have celebrated this historic moment with a public address.

In December 1989, George H. W. met with Mikhail Gorbachev, leader of the Soviet Union. They discussed reducing arms and strengthening relations between the two countries. In a 1990 summit, George H. W. and Gorbachev signed a preliminary arms-reduction agreement. Each country agreed to decrease its supply of nuclear weapons. In 1991, George H. W. and Gorbachev met in Moscow and signed the finalized agreement, called the Strategic Arms Reduction Treaty. This was the first treaty to provide significant nuclear arms reductions in both countries. The two leaders were able to improve US-Soviet relations in ways that would not have been possible only a decade earlier.

Persian Gulf War

On August 2, 1990, Iraq invaded Kuwait. Iraqi President Saddam Hussein wanted Kuwait's land, wealth, and oil, but the invasion violated international law. The UN Security Council passed Resolution 660, which condemned the invasion and demanded Iraq withdraw immediately.

George H. W.'s administration quickly went to work assembling a coalition of countries to convince Iraq to withdraw from Kuwait. The United States also placed pressure on Iraq with economic sanctions, freezing Iraqi and Kuwait assets held in US banks. In August 1990, George H. W. ordered Operation Desert Shield. The order prepared US troops to become part of an international coalition if war was necessary. George H. W. authorized an increase in US troops and resources in the Persian Gulf.

After months of diplomatic efforts, Iraqi forces remained in Kuwait. George H. W. became increasingly convinced diplomacy alone would not convince Hussein to leave Kuwait. He did not want a war, but he felt it was inevitable. On November 29, 1990, the UN Security Council authorized the use of all means necessary to remove Iraqi forces from Kuwait. The council gave January 16, 1991, as a deadline for Iraq to leave Kuwait. On January 12, 1991, Congress authorized George H. W. to use US troops in the impending conflict.

The UN deadline came and passed with no movement from Iraqi troops. On January 17, George H. W. gave the order for US troops to lead a coalition of

> **"We have no argument with the people of Iraq. Indeed, for the innocents caught in this conflict, I pray for their safety. Our goal is not the conquest of Iraq. It is the liberation of Kuwait. It is my hope that somehow the Iraqi people can, even now, convince their dictator that he must lay down his arms, leave Kuwait, and let Iraq itself rejoin the family of peace-loving nations."[9]**
> *—President George H. W. Bush, January 16, 1991*

international troops in an attack on the Iraqi army. The attack began with a massive bombing of Iraqi forces. Then the coalition launched a ground assault on February 24 and quickly forced the Iraqi army to withdraw from Kuwait. Coalition troops reached Kuwait City by February 27 and called a ceasefire on February 28. Iraqi generals surrendered on March 3. Operation Desert Storm ended in less than two months with minimal US casualties.

The Persian Gulf War demonstrated what George H. W. called the "New World Order."[10] It showed the possibility of peaceful nations joining together to stop aggressive countries. George H. W. successfully built the international coalition that provided troops and money for the operation. Critics, however, said the mission was not completed because the coalition allowed Hussein to stay in power. Some believed George H. W. should have ordered troops to pursue Hussein and remove him from power. Yet George H. W. said from the beginning his goal was to remove Iraqi forces from Kuwait. In his view, they had achieved that goal.

Bid for a Second Term

After the Persian Gulf War ended, George H. W.'s public approval ratings soared. In some polls, his approval ratings were nearly 90 percent.[11] In just one year, however, this popularity disappeared. Although George H. W. claimed several foreign policy

George H. W. visits with troops in Saudi Arabia on Thanksgiving Day 1990.

successes, many Americans were more concerned with issues facing their own country. The US economy had slowed since President Reagan's time. Middle-class Americans felt George H. W. had done little to address the country's economic problems. Beginning in July 1990 and lasting until March 1991, the country fell into recession. Many people, including white-collar workers in middle-management positions, lost their jobs. In addition, the federal deficit grew larger, driven by rising health-care spending. George H. W. was unwilling to extend unemployment benefits because he believed it would further increase the budget deficit, which made him appear unsympathetic to average Americans. More people began to believe George H. W. was out of touch with average Americans and the middle class. Recovery from the recession was slow, with unemployment rates reaching 8 percent in June 1992.[12]

Less than two years after his Persian Gulf victory, George H. W. lost the 1992 presidential election to Arkansas Governor Bill Clinton. George H. W. had come into office promising to keep the country much the same as it was during the Reagan years. However, the economy fell into recession, and Americans quickly grew dissatisfied. George H. W.'s achievements in foreign policy could not overcome the people's upset over the economy. During the presidential campaign, Clinton hammered this point home with the slogan, "It's the Economy, Stupid."[13] In addition, when George H. W. broke his pledge not to increase taxes, he angered many conservatives, costing him their support. A disorganized campaign also cost

George H. W. Lee Atwater, the strategist behind George H. W.'s successful 1988 campaign, died of brain cancer in 1991. Many believe his absence contributed to George H. W.'s defeat.

After the Presidency

After George H. W. left the White House, he and Barbara returned to Houston. They settled into private life and once again became active citizens in the community. George H. W. volunteered at church and took positions on several boards. He also worked on opening a library featuring official documents and private papers from his career. In 1997, the George Bush Presidential Library and Museum was dedicated on the west campus of Texas A&M University in College Station, Texas.

George H. W. and Barbara continued to be politically active after leaving the White House.

Following the library's dedication, George H. W. became involved with George W. and Jeb's political campaigns. After the presidential election in 2000, George H. W. and George W. became the second father and son duo to hold the office of president, along with John Adams and John Quincy Adams.

THE BIG MOMENT

ELECTION NIGHT 1992

On November 3, 1992, the Bush family gathered in a suite at the Houstonian Hotel. At a similar gathering four years earlier, the room was filled with anticipation of victory. This night, however, the mood was much more solemn. As the election night returns came in, the room grew quieter. When the final numbers confirmed Clinton's victory in the presidential election, George H. W. sat stunned. He never fully believed he would lose the election. It was a stinging defeat, one that haunted George H. W. for many years. George H. W. called Clinton shortly after the polls closed on the West Coast and conceded the election. Family members quietly got dressed up to attend the president's concession speech. As they headed for the Westin Galleria Hotel in Houston, George H. W. looked at his family members, telling them it was time to go out with style and dignity. Later, in January 1993, when Bill and Hillary Clinton arrived at the White House on

Inauguration Day, the president and Barbara received them with kindness and warmth. George H. W. wrote a letter to his successor that he left on the desk in the Oval Office. In the letter, George H. W. wished Clinton happiness and told him he was rooting for him.

CHAPTER 5

GEORGE W. BUSH

George W. Bush was born in 1946, the same year his father finished his second year at Yale University. When George W. was two years old, the family moved from New England to Texas to take advantage of the oil boom. Within a few years, George W. became a big brother when his sister Robin was born in 1949. Four years later, in 1953, brother Jeb was born. But that same year, tragedy struck the Bush family. Robin was diagnosed with advanced leukemia, which was nearly always fatal at the time. George H. W. and Barbara did not want to worry their young son, so they did not tell him much about his sister's illness. When Robin died, George W. asked why they had not told him she was so sick, a question his parents were unable to answer.

George W. with his father on the Yale campus in 1947

The tight-knit Bush family helped each other through the difficult time after Robin's death.

After Robin's death, the Bush house was a gloomy and sad place. George W. was determined to cheer up his parents, especially his mother. He became a comedian and performer. "You look around and see your parents suffering so deeply and try to be cheerful and funny, and you end up becoming a bit of a clown," said Elsie Walker, a Bush cousin.[1] Barbara remembers George W. did his best to take care of her during this time. One day when a friend called on George W. to play, he said no and explained he was going to play with his lonely mother instead. "I was thinking, 'Well, I'm being there for him,'" Barbara remembered later. "But the truth was he was being there for me."[2]

Time and the addition of three more siblings eased the pain of Robin's death for George W. and his parents. However, it left an indelible effect on George W.'s attitude and approach to life. He learned to live in the moment. According to his younger brother Marvin, George W. takes life as it meets him, without looking to the past, and without worrying about what the future holds.

School Days

Similar to many of his peers, George W. dreamed of becoming a major league baseball player. As a child, George W. played for the Midland Little League, and he went on to play baseball while attending college. Although he was not as gifted at baseball as his father and grandfather, classmates remember he was always ready to play.

In high school, George W. followed his father's path by attending boarding school in Andover. Like his father, he was well liked by classmates. He organized an informal stickball league and played on the junior varsity basketball team, although he was not a standout player.

After graduating from Andover in 1964, George W. enrolled at Yale University. According to most accounts, he was an average student, earning solid Cs. Although he did not excel at schoolwork, he showed other skills that would serve him well in the future. When pledging the Delta Kappa Epsilon fraternity, pledges were asked to name the other 55 pledges. Most could name approximately six pledges. George W. was able to name everyone in the room. Lanny J. Davis, a political adviser, said,

> There are times when George coasted through Yale courses and through exams or seemed overly facetious. But don't mistake that for not being intellectually acute. My memory of George . . . is that he was an astute observer of people and had an incredible talent for getting along with people. I tell my fellow Democrats not to underestimate him.[3]

Texas Air National Guard

George W. graduated from Yale in 1968. At the time, the Vietnam War was taking place. He joined the Texas Air National Guard and was assigned to the 147th Fighter-Interceptor Group. Some people questioned his choice to join the National Guard and criticized him for trying to dodge the draft. At the time, hundreds of US soldiers were dying in combat each week. The National Guard unit gave George W. a way to fulfill his military commitment while staying in Texas. Many young men saw service in the National Guard as a way to escape Vietnam. Although the National Guard usually had a long list of applicants, George W. was accepted immediately. Some people believe it was due to his family's political connections in Texas. George W. has maintained he did not join the National Guard to avoid action in Vietnam but because he wanted to be a fighter pilot instead of an infantry soldier.

During his first two years in the National Guard, George W. trained at flight schools in Georgia and Texas. Once he finished his two years of flight training, he drifted in and out of several jobs, not entirely sure of what he wanted to do with his life. In 1973, George W. was honorably discharged from the National Guard and moved to Boston to attend Harvard Business School.

Harvard Business School

Although many of his Harvard classmates sought careers on Wall Street, 27-year-old George W. had a different goal—he planned to return to Texas after graduating. While at Harvard, George W. was known for driving a messy car, listening to Latin country music, and chewing tobacco in class. Classmate Marty Kahn said,

George W. agreed to spend nearly two years in flight training and an additional four years in part-time service in the National Guard.

FAMILY MAN

In 1977, friends fixed up George W. with Laura Welch, a public school librarian from Midland. Although they had attended the same middle school in Midland and lived in the same apartment building in Houston, the two had never met. "I met her in the backyard at Joe and Jan O'Neill's in Midland, Texas," remembers George W. "It was the classic backyard barbeque. O'Neill said, come on over, I think you'll find somebody who might interest you. So I said, all right, popped over there. There's only four of us there, and not only did she interest me, I guess you could say it was love at first sight."[6] George W. and Laura were married only four months later. The family expanded in 1981, when Laura gave birth to twins Barbara and Jenna.

One of my first recollections of him was sitting in class and hearing the unmistakable sound of someone spitting tobacco. I turned around and there was George sitting in the back of the room in his [National Guard] bomber jacket spitting in a cup. You have to remember this was Harvard Business School. You just didn't see that kind of thing.[4]

Many people, including his mother, believe Harvard deeply influenced George W. The school's academic demands required him to think about his life and focus on his future. "Harvard was a great turning point for him. I don't think he'd say that as much as I would," said Barbara. "I think he learned, what is that word? Structure."[5]

After he graduated from Harvard Business School, George W. returned to Texas and turned his attention to making his fortune in the oil business, as his father had before him. In 1977, he formed Arbusto Energy, which changed its name to Bush Exploration in 1982. George W. earned a reputation as a party-loving bachelor. That changed in 1977, when he met and married Laura Welch after a four-month whirlwind romance. When oil prices fell, Bush Exploration struggled. It merged with a smaller oil firm and was acquired by Harken Energy Corporation in 1986.

Texas Politics

As had his father and grandfather, George W. felt the urge to dip his feet into political waters. He made his first campaign in 1978, running for US representative from Texas's Nineteenth Congressional District. He lost to Kent Hance. George W. helped with his father's 1988 presidential campaign, serving as a campaign adviser and media liaison.

In 1994, George W. entered the campaign arena again, throwing his hat in the ring for Texas governor. He was not fond of the incumbent, Richards, who had mocked his father at the 1988 DNC and insulted his upper-class background. Richards also made

> **"I think his political philosophy comes completely from the philosophy of the independent oil man. His homage to his parents, his respect for his elders, his respect for tradition, his belief in religion, his opposition to abortion— that's the philosophy he grew up with here."[7]**
>
> *—Joe O'Neill, childhood friend of George W. Bush*

TEXAS RANGERS

With some of the money George W. received from the Harken Energy buyout, he organized a group of investors to buy the Texas Rangers, a major league baseball team, in 1989. George W. served as the team's managing general partner for the next five years. He and his group of investors put together a deal that helped build a modern ballpark in Arlington, Texas, and paid for it with local and state government funding. The investment in the Rangers made George W. a rich man, earning him $15 million on an original investment of $600,000.[10] George W. gained the respect of his staff and other baseball team owners. Employees and players say he was easy to talk to, often having conversations in Spanish with the Hispanic players.

fun of George W., calling him "Shrub."[8] Listening to his advisers, George W. refrained from responding to Richards in the same way. He insisted on referring to her only as Governor Richards. For months, the race was close, but in the weeks before Election Day, George W. pulled into the lead. He defeated Richards and became Texas's forty-sixth governor.

Once in the Texas statehouse, George W.'s likeable personality and his willingness to give people credit for their contributions carried him far. He worked with Texas Democrats to form large working legislative majorities that passed laws in many areas. In 1998, Texas voters reelected the popular governor in a landslide over Democrat Gary Mauro. In the election, George W. won 239 out of 254 counties in Texas.[9]

Republicans around the country began taking notice of the "new" Bush leading Texas. Whispers swirled of a presidential run in 2000. On March 7, 1999, George W. announced he had created a presidential exploratory committee, saying:

> I believe in the promise of America—the fundamentally American conviction that each of us can be what we want to be, can achieve what we want to achieve, so long as we are willing to work and earn it. The promise is meant for everyone, not just a few—and as we move into the 21st century, I want the party of Lincoln to be the party that makes sure no one is left behind.[11]

"More than almost any other candidate in history, I understood what running for president would entail. . . . I knew how hard it was to win. And I knew how much it hurt to lose."[12]

—George W. Bush, on running for president

George W.'s presidential exploratory committee stands behind him as he makes his announcement on March 7.

CHAPTER 6

RETURN TO THE WHITE HOUSE

In June 1999, George W. announced he would run for president of the United States and vowed to be a "compassionate conservative."[1] In the summer of 2000, George W. easily won the Republican Party nomination. In his acceptance speech at the Republican National Convention, George W. promised to set a new tone in Washington, DC, which had been tangled in recent years by an impeachment fight between Clinton and House Republicans. "I have no stake in the bitter arguments of the last few years," George W. said in his nomination acceptance speech. "I want to change the tone of Washington to one of civility and respect."[2]

George W.'s opponent in the election was Vice President Al Gore. The race between the two men was very close. Gore had experience

George W. celebrated with his wife, Laura, after he delivered his acceptance speech at the Republican National Convention in 2000.

and expertise in politics, in particular foreign policy. But he sometimes appeared patronizing and impatient toward George W., which did not help his public image. As Americans headed to the polls on November 7, 2000, the race was razor tight.

As the returns came in on election night, the race was too close to call. Gore had won the East and West Coasts and inland industrial cities. George W. had taken many of the Midwest, plains, and southern states. Eventually, it became clear the winner would be the man who won the state of Florida. At first, television networks projected Gore had won Florida and declared him the winner. However, as more Florida districts reported results, the election became too close to call. Then the television networks declared George W. the winner. At one point on election night, Gore conceded the victory to George W., only to later revoke his concession when it became apparent the race in Florida was still too close to call. Only a few hundred votes separated the two candidates. Over the next five weeks, there were vote recounts and lawsuits. Bitter disputes erupted over election procedures, confusing ballots, and partially punched voting cards. In the end, recounts found George W. won Florida by only 537 votes. The official outcome of the election was not decided until December 12, 2000, when the US Supreme Court certified Florida's electoral votes, awarding the state to George W. Although Gore received approximately 500,000 more popular votes than George W. nationwide, George W. won the Electoral College 271 to 266.[3] It was the

Jeb celebrates with George W. after the initial election results came in on November 7.

first time since Benjamin Harrison in 1888 that a candidate won the electoral vote but lost the popular vote.

After a hard-fought election, a vote recount, and a Supreme Court decision, the George W. family achieved one of the rarest accomplishments in US politics—a father and son who both served as president of the United States.

ELECTORAL COLLEGE

The Electoral College is a group of 538 voters who determine the president and vice president of the United States. When citizens vote in presidential elections, they are choosing which candidate will receive their state's electoral votes. In 48 states, the candidate who wins the most votes receives all of that state's electoral votes. In Maine and Nebraska, electoral votes are allocated based on the number of votes in each congressional district. A majority of 270 electoral votes is needed to elect a president.[4] The Electoral College system was designed by the country's founding fathers. It was a compromise between those who wanted members of Congress to elect the president and those who believed the president should be elected by a popular vote of citizens.

Becoming President

On January 20, 2001, George W. was sworn in as the forty-third president of the United States. He took the oath of office 12 years after his father had done so. In the early days of his presidency, George W. focused on domestic issues. He made proposals to cut taxes and expand energy production. He also focused on education issues. His first major initiative was the No Child Left Behind Act of 2001. It created reforms aimed at raising standards and improving test scores at the country's public schools. George W. increased the size of Pell Grants to help college students pay for school and created the Helping America's Youth Initiative, which connected adults with at-risk children who may have trouble transitioning

NO CHILD LEFT BEHIND ACT

When he took office in 2000, George W. developed a plan to reform public school education. In 2002, George W. signed the No Child Left Behind Act into law after it passed the House and Senate with large margins. If schools do not meet performance standards, they have to take specific, concrete steps to improve in order to receive federal funding.

Although the Democrats overwhelmingly supported the passage of the bill, some expressed concerns there was not enough funding to implement it properly.

Massachusetts Senator Edward Kennedy called out George W.'s administration's funding allocations for education, saying it was much less than the administration had promised. These criticisms increased over time, and by the 2004 campaign, Kerry used the No Child Left Behind Act as an example of a broken promise from the president. George W. countered by saying he had increased Department of Education spending by approximately 49 percent.[5]

successfully into adulthood. In the program, adults served as positive role models and mentors to support youth. Although George W. was tackling several domestic issues in his first months as president, he would soon face a bigger challenge.

George W.'s presidency was forever changed on the morning of September 11, 2001. Terrorists hijacked four commercial airplanes, crashing two into the World Trade Center buildings in New York City and a third into the Pentagon in Arlington, Virginia. Passengers on the fourth hijacked plane fought back, and during the struggle, the plane crashed into a field near Shanksville, Pennsylvania.

THE BIG MOMENT

UNIFYING A NATION

On September 11, 2001, George W. was reading to a classroom full of children in Sarasota, Florida. Chief of Staff Andrew Card quietly approached and whispered into the president's ear. A plane had hit the World Trade Center Towers in New York City. The United States was under attack. Although horror flashed across the president's face, he carried on for the young students as if nothing was wrong. He did not want to create any panic among the children or the surrounding press corps while the situation was so shaky. After finishing the lesson, he thanked the teacher and students and left the room. Immediately, he went to a holding room where aides were gathering as much information as possible. The country felt unsettled as rumors flew about possible future attacks and targets.

Three days later, on September 14, George W. flew to New York City. He stood at Ground Zero where the rubble of the World Trade Center

George W. comforts a firefighter as they stand atop the rubble of the World Trade Center Towers in New York City.

Towers smoldered. As he toured the devastation, George W. climbed on top of the rubble and put his arm around a tired firefighter. He grabbed a bullhorn and began thanking firefighters and other first responders at the scene. When someone in the crowd shouted they could not hear him, George W. shouted, "I can hear you! The rest of the world hears you! And the people—and the people who knocked these buildings down will hear all of us soon."[6] In that unscripted and instinctive moment, George W. found his voice as a leader, delivering the message Americans needed to hear and, in the process, unifying a nation.

The damage to the World Trade Center Towers caused the two buildings to collapse, killing thousands of civilians, firefighters, and emergency medical personnel. It was the deadliest terrorist attack on US soil.

Three days after the attack, George W. visited New York City. He was shocked by the horror of the scene. "As we approached Ground Zero, I felt like I was entering a nightmare. There was little light. Smoke hung in the air mixed with suspended particles of debris, creating an eerie gray curtain. . . . They had hit us harder than I comprehended."[7]

"Terrorist attacks can shake the foundations of our biggest buildings, but they cannot touch the foundation of America. These acts shattered steel, but they cannot dent the steel of American resolve. America was targeted for attack because we're the brightest beacon for freedom and opportunity in the world. And no one will keep that light from shining."[8]
—President George W. Bush, September 11, 2001

War on Terror

In response to the September 11 terrorist attacks, George W. declared a war on terrorism. The United States entered into a worldwide assault on terrorists and those who supported terrorist activities. The CIA believed Osama bin Laden, the leader of terrorist organization al-Qaeda, was behind the attacks. Bin Laden had taken refuge in Afghanistan, where the Taliban, a fundamentalist Islamic group, had allowed him to stay. On September 20, George W.

LAURA'S LITERACY WORK

Laura Bush worked as a librarian and elementary school teacher in Texas before marrying George W. in 1977. As First Lady, Laura focused on literacy and education initiatives. Working with the Library of Congress, Laura created the National Book Festival in 2001. This annual festival takes place in Washington, DC, on the National Mall, attracting thousands of people. Laura and George W. also hosted the White House Conference on Global Literacy in 2006. They wanted to encourage reading throughout the world. Laura continued her work with literacy programs, including creating the Laura Bush Foundation for America's Libraries and writing a book called *Read All About It!* with daughter Jenna Bush Hager.

spoke to members of Congress. He demanded the Taliban surrender bin Laden and all al-Qaeda leaders in Afghanistan to the United States. George W.'s foreign policy advisers and the CIA told him this was highly unlikely to happen.

On October 7, the United States struck terrorist camps in Afghanistan with missile attacks, and the war began. US forces were joined with troops from the United Kingdom, along with support from other nations, such as France, Germany, Australia, and Canada. Partnering with an Afghani anti-Taliban rebel force called the Northern Alliance, US forces defeated the Taliban in Afghanistan and helped set up a fragile democracy. Bin Laden, however, managed to evade capture.

George W. speaks outside the White House with a team of advisers on their plan to boost the US economy after the September 11 attacks.

As part of the war on terrorism, George W. reorganized the federal government to deal with modern-day terror threats. He established the National Counterterrorism Center, the Department of Homeland Security, the Homeland Security Council, and a new position for the Director of National Intelligence.

Iraq War

After the Afghanistan invasion, George W.'s administration turned its attention to an old enemy, Iraqi leader Hussein. Although Iraq had not been linked to the September 11 attacks, the United States was nervous about the nation's intentions. Armed with intelligence reports that later proved to be incorrect, many officials in George W.'s administration, including Vice President Dick Cheney and Deputy Secretary of Defense Paul Wolfowitz, believed Iraq was building large supplies of biological and chemical weapons. They also thought Iraq was attempting to develop nuclear weapons. George W.'s administration feared Iraq was likely to supply terrorists with these weapons of mass destruction (WMDs) and said Hussein had direct ties to al-Qaeda. Administration officials thought the United States should end the threat once and for all by removing Hussein from power.

On January 29, 2002, George W. addressed the issue of Iraq and WMDs in his State of the Union address. He said the United States would not allow Hussein to acquire these nuclear weapons. Over the next year, George W.'s administration built the case to remove Hussein from power. In October, George W. presented Congress with a resolution

> **"On my orders, the United States military has begun strikes against Al-Qaeda terrorist training camps and military installations of the Taliban regime in Afghanistan."[10]**
>
> **—President George W. Bush, October 7, 2001**

that authorized US forces to invade Iraq if Hussein did not surrender his WMDs. The resolution passed by a wide margin in both the House of Representatives and the Senate.

Some people feared the United States was rushing into a war and that Iraq was not a threat. They suggested using UN sanctions and other measures to make Hussein turn over his WMDs. They said there was no proof an Iraqi attack was planned. George W. gathered international support against Iraq. On November 8, the UN Security Council voted to authorize weapons inspectors in Iraq and promised "serious consequences" if Iraq did not comply with the inspectors' requests.[9]

September 11 had taught George W. that no one can ever know when an attack will occur. "Some have said that we must not act until the threat is imminent," George W. explained in his January 28, 2003, State of the Union address. "But trusting in the sanity and restraint of Saddam Hussein is not a strategy and it is not an option."[11]

On March 17, George W. gave a nationally televised speech in which he gave Hussein 48 hours to resign. After no sign of Hussein leaving power, on March 19, the invasion of Iraq began. The Iraq War lasted for almost a decade. In its first phase, a combined force of US and British troops, along with support from several other countries, invaded Iraq and defeated its military. In a longer second phase, the United

States led an occupation of the country that was opposed by Iraqi insurgents. This phase also removed Hussein from power.

The decision to invade Iraq became one of the most controversial choices of George W.'s administration. Although the Iraq War achieved its goal of toppling Hussein's government, no evidence of WMDs was found. In addition, the war was very costly in lives and dollars for the United States.

BEHIND THE SCENES
WARRIOR 100K

Every spring since 2010, George W. hops on his bike for the Warrior 100K. Approximately 20 servicemen and women who have been wounded in the war on terrorism join him. Together, they embark on a 100-kilometer (62 mile) bike ride over three days, sharing experiences with each other as they ride. The ride honors service members injured in Iraq and Afghanistan.

The Warrior 100K is part of the George W. Bush Institute's Military Service Initiative program. The program was established to honor post–September 11 veterans and to provide support as they transition home from service. According to George W., the ride is a great way to highlight the work of nonprofits and other companies committed to helping US veterans. In addition to the Warrior 100K, in the fall, the Military Service Initiative hosts an annual golf tournament for veterans.

IRAQ SURGE IN 2007

By 2006, Iraq was in chaos as fighting intensified between different groups of Iraqis. Many Americans believed the United States should withdraw its troops. Instead, George W. announced a plan in January 2007 to send in a surge of more than 20,000 additional troops to reduce violence in the country.[14] After the surge, the violence in Iraq declined significantly, and many supporters claimed success. Others disagreed, pointing out that as the United States began withdrawing troops in the years since 2007, the country has remained in turmoil with an increase in civil war fighting.

The 2004 Election

In 2004, George W. ran for reelection. He faced Senator John Kerry from Massachusetts. The Iraq War became one of the central issues in the election. Senator Kerry argued George W. had made a great error in judgment in invading Iraq. George W. defended his decision, saying, "I think it's worth it because I know in the long term, a free Iraq, a free Afghanistan will set such a powerful example in a part of the world that's so desperate for freedom. It will change the world so we can look back and say we did our duty."[12]

Many Americans agreed with George W.'s decision, and he was reelected for a second term. Although he had enjoyed high public approval ratings during his first term, his popularity sank during his second term. Critics blasted George W. for invading Iraq on what proved to be false reports of WMDs. In addition, when

Hurricane Katrina devastated the Gulf Coast in 2005, many criticized George W.'s administration for a slow response.

American mood had also soured because of the troubling state of the economy. When George W. first took office in 2001, there was a federal budget surplus. However, the cost of fighting two wars, along with widespread tax cuts implemented during his first term, created annual budget deficits, beginning in 2002. Adding to the public's dissatisfaction, in 2008, the United States faced its worst financial crisis since the Great Depression. Congress passed a series of plans sponsored by George W.'s administration to bail out the financial industry, which would cost billions of dollars. By the time he left office in 2009, George W.'s approval rating had sunk to 22 percent, according to a CBS/New York Times poll.[13]

Despite his high approval ratings going into his second term, Americans became more unhappy with George W. during his last years as president.

CHAPTER 7

JEB BUSH

Born on February 11, 1953, in Midland, John Ellis "Jeb" Bush was the third child of George and Barbara. He lived in Midland for six years before moving to Houston. In 1966, his father was elected as a US representative, and the family traveled between Texas and Washington, DC.

In 1967, 14-year-old Jeb headed to Andover to attend Phillips Academy, as his father and brother had done. Many expected Jeb to fit right in with Andover's elite world. Jeb, however, was different from his brother and father. He had little in common with his father, a star on the Andover campus, and was an even worse student than his brother. Jeb refused to join the campus Republicans club and often appeared

Jeb, *right*, with older brother, George W., in 1955

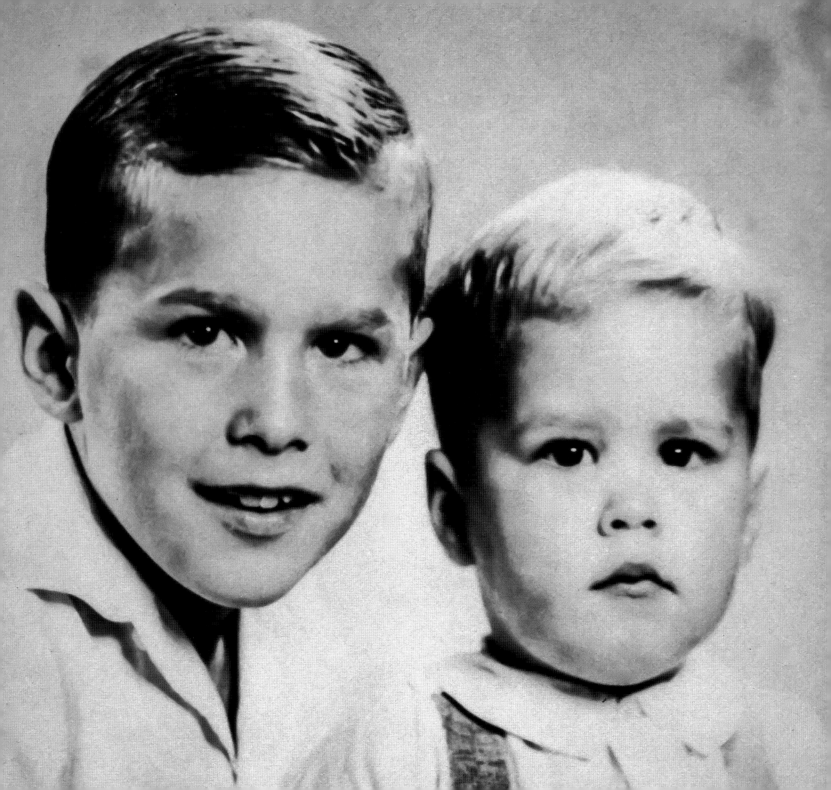

detached to those around him. "He was just in a bit of a different world," said classmate Phil Sylvester. While other students "were constantly arguing about politics and particularly Vietnam, he just wasn't interested, he didn't participate, he didn't care."[1]

According to many accounts, Andover was a difficult place for a teenager. "It was a very, very tough competitive environment," said Paul Anderson, a classmate who recalls Jeb as being aloof and sometimes uncomfortable at the school. "I look back at it, even after all this time, as being more difficult socially and academically than college."[2] Jeb says his grades were so poor he was in danger of being expelled at one point. He also says his time at Andover was one of the hardest periods in his life, and he was known to drink alcohol and smoke marijuana, acts that could have led to his expulsion from the school.

Jeb struggled during his high school years at Phillips Academy.

Life-Changing Trip

In 1971, Jeb took a school trip to central Mexico. The trip was meant to introduce students to another culture while the Andover boys helped build a schoolhouse. On the trip, 17-year-old Jeb met a Mexican girl named Columba Gallo. He says it was love at first sight. "I literally fell in love with my now-wife of 44 years that Sunday afternoon in that plaza of Leon," he says.[3] When he returned to Andover, Jeb wrote to Columba constantly. Friends noticed a change in him. Before the Mexico trip, Jeb was more casual, but after the trip, he became more serious.

In 1971, after his high school graduation, Jeb registered for the draft. As the Vietnam War was winding down, however, he was not drafted. Instead, he enrolled at the University of Texas in Austin, where he majored in Latin American studies. In 1973, Jeb graduated early from his program and married Columba in 1974. They eventually had three children: George P., Noelle, and John Ellis Jr.

Early Career

After college, Jeb started his career in business, working for Texas Commerce Bank. He spent two years in Caracas, Venezuela, opening a branch for the bank. In 1980, Jeb and his family returned to the United States so he could work on his father's first presidential campaign. After the election, Jeb moved his family to Miami, Florida, where he worked as a real estate developer and real estate agent.

FAMILY TROUBLES

Over the years, Jeb's daughter Noelle has struggled with drug addiction. In 2002, she was arrested and charged with fraudulently buying prescription drugs. She was sentenced to a drug rehabilitation program. While at the facility, she was caught with stolen pills and was sentenced to two days in jail. Two months later, she was caught hiding crack cocaine in her shoe at the same facility. This time, the judge ordered her to serve ten days in jail. At the time, Jeb was in the midst of campaigning for reelection as Florida's governor. While he supported Noelle throughout her court appearances, he also stated she needed to accept responsibility for her actions and make the necessary changes in her life. In 2003, Noelle graduated from a drug rehabilitation program and began moving forward with her life. Noelle's drug problems have inspired Columba to become involved with several organizations that advocate for the treatment and prevention of substance abuse.

In Florida, Jeb became more involved in politics and was elected chairman of the Dade County Republican Party. In 1987 and 1988, he served as Florida's secretary of commerce, his first government post. In 1988, Jeb resigned the post to work on his father's successful presidential campaign.

Florida Governor

In 1994, Jeb ran for governor of Florida. He won the Republican nomination for Florida governor but lost the general election by a small margin to the Democratic incumbent, Lawton Chiles. After his defeat, Jeb threw himself into his work with Florida charities and civic groups. He founded a nonprofit public policy organization called the

Foundation for Florida's Future and cofounded Florida's first charter school, a school that receives public funding but operates independently of the local school system.

In 1998, Jeb entered the race for the Florida governor's office again. His connections and popularity with Florida's Hispanic community helped him in the election. Not only was he married to a Hispanic woman, but he also had deep ties to Latin-American and Cuban businesses in Florida. This time he won, defeating Democratic Lieutenant Governor Buddy MacKay.

As governor, Jeb reached out to form alliances with other minority communities in Florida, primarily through a serious commitment to improving Florida's inner-city schools. He emphasized the importance of parental involvement in education.

As governor of Florida, Jeb found himself tangled in the 2000 presidential election controversy. Florida's votes would determine the outcome of the election. Because his brother George W. was

ENVIRONMENTAL LEGACY

While serving as Florida governor, Jeb initiated several environmental improvements. In 2000, he signed the Everglades Restoration Act into law. The act established an $8 billion restoration plan for Florida's Everglades. In addition, Jeb set aside more than 1 million acres (400,000 ha) of land for conservation through a land-buying program.[4] In 2003, Jeb signed an amendment to Florida's 1994 Everglades Forever Act that extended pollution cleanup requirements for the Everglades until 2016.

running against Gore, Jeb excused himself from participating in any decisions related to the election. He was determined to avoid the appearance of improper behavior because of his family connection.

In 2002, Jeb ran for a second term as governor. Many doubted he would win because no Republican had ever won reelection in Florida. Jeb, however, was extremely popular with Floridians and was reelected. In 2006, Florida law prohibited Jeb from running for a third straight term. As a result, Jeb left the governor's office in 2007, after serving in the position for eight years. A popular governor, Jeb is credited with many efforts to improve the state's education system, protect the environment, and improve the state economy.

Presidential Ambitions

Since leaving the governor's office, Jeb has remained active in several political issues. He has supported educational initiatives, in particular the Common Core Standards, which define what students in each grade should know in English and math. He has also supported immigration reform efforts. His name was linked to the 2008 Senate race and the 2012 presidential election, but he ultimately decided not to run in either race.

For Republicans who have struggled to attract minority and Hispanic voters, many view Jeb as uniquely positioned to win over these voters. He is a popular two-time governor of Florida, a state heavily populated with Hispanic voters. He has a record of improving education for minorities, is fluent in Spanish, and is married to a Hispanic woman.

In December 2014, Jeb announced on his Facebook page that he was actively exploring the potential of running for president of the United States in 2016. He launched a political action committee in January 2015. And on June 15, 2015, he officially announced his candidacy. Many people believe Jeb is one of the leading candidates for the Republican nomination for president. If he succeeds, the Bush family will become the only US family in history to have three members serve as president of the United States.

"When the idea of Jeb running for President first came up, I was hesitant. . . . But our problems are so profound that America needs a leader who can renew the promise of this great nation."[5]
—*Barbara Bush, February 2015*

Jeb's popularity among Hispanic voters is an advantage other Republican candidates may not have.

THE FUTURE OF THE BUSH FAMILY

CHAPTER 8

In March 2014, George P. Bush, Jeb's son, won the Republican nomination for Texas land commissioner. His victory announced the arrival of the next generation of Bush politicians. This great-grandson of a senator, grandson and nephew of two presidents, and son of a governor was ready to launch his own campaign.

George P. has been hailed as the heir to the Bush political dynasty since his birth in 1976. At age 12, he spoke at the first RNC that nominated his grandfather, George H. W. At age 24, he recorded television commercials for his uncle George W.'s 2000 presidential campaign, saying, "I have an uncle who is running for president because

George P. has been in the political spotlight since he gave a speech at the 1992 RNC.

he believes in . . . opportunity for every American, for every Latino. His name? The same as mine, George Bush."[1]

After graduating from Rice University in Houston with a history degree, George P. taught in an inner-city high school. Later, he went to law school and served in the US Navy in Afghanistan. He has also worked as a political fund raiser for the Republican Party, helping reach out to Latinos and the younger generation of Americans.

According to Ana Navarro, a Republican consultant in Florida who is close to Jeb, George P. has a promising political future. She says he is "the real deal and a complete package—has intellect, personality, good looks, business experience, military service, is bilingual and half Hispanic, and the family connections don't hurt."[2]

In November 2014, George P. accomplished a Bush family first, winning the first election he ran in, an accomplishment his great-grandfather, grandfather, uncle, and father could not match. He won the Texas land commissioner election over the Democratic candidate, former El Paso, Texas, Mayor John Cook. As Texas land commissioner, George P. advocated for military veterans, administered Texas's publicly held lands, and oversaw mineral rights for oil and gas companies. His office also controlled revenues from the oil and gas industry, which contribute to the Permanent School Fund, the country's largest educational endowment. Although the four-year post is not well-known, it is a powerful position in Texas politics that

With his experience, George P. has a bright political future.

offers experience and connections George P. could use to elevate himself to higher offices in the future. US Representative Roger Williams commended George P. at his swearing-in ceremony in January 2015, saying, "This man will be much more than a land commissioner. He'll be a leader."[3]

> **"My family has always said . . . if you're going to get into politics, do it for the right reasons, not because you've got to carry on something."[4]**
>
> —*George P. Bush*

Jeb Bush Jr.

Jeb's second son, Jeb Jr., may also one day have a future in politics. Born in 1983, Jeb Jr. earned a bachelor's degree in Latin American studies from the University of Texas in Austin. In 2008, he graduated with a master's degree in international real estate finance from Florida International University. As many Bush family members before him, Jeb Jr. works in business and real estate, serving as the chief operating officer at Jeb Bush & Associates. This consulting firm specializes in business development and strategic advisory services, helping companies better grow and operate their businesses. He also serves as a managing partner for a Texas-based oil and gas service business. Jeb Jr. is involved in numerous community and charity organizations, including Sunpac, a Florida-based Hispanic outreach program. He is a board member for several organizations, including the charter school Intervisual, the Hispanic Business Initiative Fund, and the National Immigration Forum. In addition, Jeb Jr. serves as the chairman of the Friends of St. Jude, a young professional organization that raises money for St. Jude Children's Hospital in Memphis, Tennessee.

Jeb Jr., right, endorses Marco Rubio for a Florida Senate seat in 2010.

JENNA BUSH HAGER

After graduating from the University of Texas in 2004 with a degree in English, Jenna Bush Hager, one of George W.'s twin daughters, began working as a teacher, author, and journalist. Following the 2004 presidential election, Jenna taught third grade at a charter school in Washington, DC. In 2006, she visited Africa with her mother and became an intern for UNICEF, teaching in Latin America and traveling to Paraguay. Her experiences inspired her to write the *New York Times* best-selling children's book *Ana's Story: A Journal of Hope*, in 2007. The story is based on the life of a 17-year-old single mother in Latin American who is infected with HIV.

Also in 2008, Jenna married Henry Chase Hager, a former White House aide. Jenna and Henry met during her father's campaign for the 2004 presidential election. Five years later, in 2013, Jenna and Henry welcomed their first child, a daughter named Margaret Laura Hager. She gave birth to another girl, Poppy Louise Hager, in 2015.

Jenna's twin, Barbara, cofounded and is CEO of Global Health Corps, a group working toward improving global health. She has also worked with the Red Cross Children's Hospital in South Africa and interned with UNICEF in various locations.

In 2013, Jeb Jr. was selected, along with lobbyist and conservative activist Slater Bayliss, to lead Maverick PAC (MavPAC) in Florida, a Republican-aligned group looking to reach out to young voters. Many Florida Republicans were pleased with Jeb Jr.'s selection. While he has not yet run for political office, Jeb Jr.'s name is often brought up as a potential candidate in future elections.

By adapting to the changing world around them, the Bushes have managed to stay relevant in US politics for decades.

Lasting Legacy

Despite all of its success, many members of the Bush family do not consider their family a dynasty. In fact, some even say the words *dynasty* and *legacy* irritate the family. Instead, the men and women of the Bush family value self-sufficiency. They were taught to make their own way in the world, instead of relying on the fortunes of those who came before them. They have established themselves as one of the United States' political dynasties through hard work and their talent for making and keeping friendships and alliances. With the promising future of the younger generation, they are positioned to have a voice in US politics for many years to come.

1895

Prescott S. Bush is born.

1924

George Herbert Walker Bush is born to Prescott and Dorothy Bush.

1944

George H. W. is shot down over the Pacific Ocean during World War II but is rescued by a US submarine.

1946

George Walker Bush is born to George H. W. and Barbara Bush.

1952

Prescott is elected to the US Senate.

1953

George H. W. and Barbara's young daughter, Robin, dies of leukemia; son Jeb Bush is born.

1966

George H. W. is elected to the US House of Representatives.

1970

George H. W. is appointed as the US ambassador to the UN.

1980

George H. W. is elected vice president of the United States, serving the next eight years with President Ronald Reagan.

1988

George H. W. is elected president of the United States.

1991

The United States and its allies launch Operation Desert Storm to drive Iraqi military out of Kuwait.

1992

Bill Clinton defeats George H. W. in the presidential election.

1994

In November, George W. wins the election for governor of Texas, while his brother Jeb loses his race for Florida governor.

1998

Jeb is elected governor of Florida where he serves two terms.

2000

George W. wins a highly contested presidential election over Vice President Al Gore.

2001

Terrorists attack the United States on September 11. The United States declares a war on terrorism and invades Afghanistan to hunt down the terrorists responsible for the attacks.

2003

The Iraq War begins and topples the Saddam Hussein regime, although no evidence of weapons of mass destruction is found.

2004

George W. wins reelection against Senator John Kerry.

2014

George P. Bush, son of Jeb and Columba Bush, wins his first election for Texas land commissioner.

2015

Jeb enters the 2016 presidential race.

- After the devastation of Hurricane Katrina, George H. W. and former president Bill Clinton formed the Bush-Clinton Katrina Fund to help victims in Louisiana.

- In 1999, George H. W. celebrated his 75th birthday by skydiving. He celebrated his 80th, 85th, and 90th birthdays the same way.

- George H. W. acted as president for eight hours while President Reagan was in surgery after being shot on July 13, 1985.

- George H. W. does not like broccoli.

- On his 40th birthday, George W. decided he would never again drink alcohol.

- George W. appointed Condoleezza Rice as secretary of state in 2005, making her the first African-American woman in a senior role in the US president's cabinet.

- George H. W.'s dog Millie, a springer spaniel, was the first presidential pet to "write" a book. In the book, Millie describes a day in her life at the White House.

- George W. began painting after leaving the White House.

- The George W. Bush Presidential Library and Museum is located on the campus of Southern Methodist University in Dallas, Texas.

- George W. and Laura traveled to Africa in 2013 to help renovate a cancer screening clinic.

- Raised as an Episcopalian, Jeb converted to Catholicism in 1995. His wife, Columba, also is a practicing Catholic.

- When George W. proposed to Laura, she said yes as long as she did not have to give a campaign speech, a condition she later relented on.

- Barbara Pierce Bush is a relative of Franklin Pierce, the fourteenth president of the United States.

- Prescott often played golf with President Dwight D. Eisenhower and refused to take it easy on him.

alliance
A union or association formed for mutual benefit, especially between countries or organizations.

aspiration
A hope or ambition of achieving a goal.

concession
Something that is granted.

conservative
One who believes in established, traditional values in politics, marked by moderation and caution, and resistance to change.

cuff link
A decorative button used to fasten a shirt cuff.

deficit
The excess of spending and liabilities over revenue and assets.

discharge
To officially release someone, such as from military service.

economy
The production, trade, and consumption of goods and services in a given geographic location.

fundamentalist
Strict observance to the principles of any set of beliefs.

incumbent
An official currently in office.

indelible
Not able to be forgotten or removed.

insurgent
A rebel or revolutionary.

integrity
The quality of being honest and having high moral standards.

liberal
One who is open to new ideas and ways of thinking, and who believes the government should be active in supporting social and political change.

mandate
The authority to carry out a policy or action.

moderate
An individual who is not extreme in his or her views.

nominate
To recommend or propose someone to run for office.

platform
The aims and principles of a political party.

recession
A period of time during which the economy slows down, including a decline in trade and industrial activity and the loss of jobs.

reform
To make changes.

sanction
An action or order given by one country to force another country to obey international laws; actions include limiting or stopping trade, or suspending economic aid.

selectman
A member of the government in small New England towns.

subsidiary
Something that is owned by another company.

sympathizer
Someone who agrees with or supports a position or opinion.

SELECTED BIBLIOGRAPHY

"American President: George Walker Bush." *Miller Center.* University of Virginia, n.d. Web. 25 June 2015.

Baker, Peter. "The Bushes, As Distinct and Alike as Brothers Can Be." *New York Times.* New York Times Company, 17 Jan. 2015. Web. 25 June 2015.

"Biography: George H. W. Bush." *American Experience.* WGBH Educational Foundation, n.d. Web. 25 June 2015.

Schweizer, Peter, and Rochelle Schweizer. *The Bushes: Portrait of a Dynasty.* New York: Doubleday, 2004. Print.

FURTHER READINGS

Bush, George W. *41: A Portrait of My Father.* New York: Crown, 2014. Print.

Heppermann, Christine. *Bush v. Gore: The Florida Recounts of the 2000 Presidential Election.* Minneapolis, MN: Abdo, 2013. Print.

WEBSITES

To learn more about America's Great Political Families, visit **booklinks.abdopublishing.com**. These links are routinely monitored and updated to provide the most current information available.

PLACES TO VISIT

GEORGE BUSH PRESIDENTIAL LIBRARY AND MUSEUM

1000 George Bush Drive

West College Station, TX 77845

979-691-4000

http://bush41.org

The George Bush Presidential Library and Museum preserves and makes available the records and artifacts of George H. W. Bush, forty-first president of the United States.

GEORGE W. BUSH PRESIDENTIAL LIBRARY AND MUSEUM

2943 SMU Boulevard

Dallas, TX 75205

214-346-1650

www.georgewbushlibrary.smu.edu

The George W. Bush Presidential Library and Museum serves as a resource for the study of the life and career of George W. Bush.

CHAPTER 1. ELECTION NIGHT 1994

1. Peter Baker. "The Bushes, As Distinct and Alike as Brothers Can Be." *New York Times*. New York Times Company, 17 Jan. 2015. Web. 25 June 2015.

2. George W. Bush. *41: A Portrait of My Father*. New York: Crown, 2014. Print. 254.

3. Peter Schweizer and Rochelle Schweizer. *The Bushes: Portrait of a Dynasty*. New York: Doubleday, 2004. Print. xii.

4. Dan Roberts. "Bush Dynasty Looks to Jeb to Run for President in 2016." *Guardian*. Guardian News and Media, 13 Nov. 2014. Web. 22 July 2015.

5. Peter Schweizer and Rochelle Schweizer. *The Bushes: Portrait of a Dynasty*. New York: Doubleday, 2004. Print. xv

6. George W. Bush. *41: A Portrait of My Father*. New York: Crown, 2014. Print. 255.

CHAPTER 2. POLITICAL BEGINNINGS

1. Peter Schweizer and Rochelle Schweizer. *The Bushes: Portrait of a Dynasty*. New York: Doubleday, 2004. Print. 1215.

2. Ibid. 129, 146.

3. Ibid. 126.

4. Ibid. 147.

CHAPTER 3. GEORGE H. W. BUSH

1. "Biography: George H. W. Bush." *American Experience*. WGBH Educational Foundation, n.d. Web. 25 June 2015.

2. Ibid.

3. "George H. W. Bush: Life before the Presidency." *Miller Center*. Rector and Visitors of University of Virginia, n.d. Web. 22 July 2015.

4. George W. Bush. *41: A Portrait of My Father*. New York: Crown, 2014. Kindle.

5. "Presidential Elections." *History*. A&E Television Networks, 2015. Web. 22 July 2015.

CHAPTER 4. THE WHITE HOUSE

1. "Program Transcript." *American Experience*. WGBH Educational Foundation, n.d. Web. 22 July 2015.

2. George H. W. Bush. "Acceptance Speech at the Republican National Convention." *Miller Center*. Rector and Visitors of University of Virginia, 18 Aug. 1988. Web. 22 July 2015.

3. Ibid.

4. "George H. W. Bush: Campaigns and Elections." *Miller Center*. Rector and Visitors of University of Virginia, n.d. Web. 22 July 2015.

5. "Program Transcript." *American Experience.* WGBH Educational Foundation, n.d. Web. 22 July 2015.

6. "George H. W. Bush: Domestic Affairs." *Miller Center.* Rector and Visitors of University of Virginia, n.d. Web. 22 July 2015.

7. "Literacy: Something to Be Thankful For." *Barbara Bush Foundation for Family Literacy.* Barbara Bush Foundation for Family Literacy, 26 Nov. 2014. Web. 22 July 2015.

8. "George H. W. Bush: Domestic Affairs." *Miller Center.* Rector and Visitors of University of Virginia, n.d. Web. 22 July 2015.

9. George H. W. Bush. "Address to the Nation on the Invasion of Iraq." *Miller Center.* Rector and Visitors of University of Virginia, 16 Jan. 1991. Web. 22 July 2015.

10. "George H. W. Bush: Foreign Affairs." *Miller Center.* Rector and Visitors of University of Virginia, n.d. Web. 22 July 2015.

11. "Biography: George H. W. Bush." *American Experience.* WGBH Educational Foundation, n.d. Web. 22 July 2015.

12. "1990–92 Early 1990s Recession." *The Bancroft Library.* Regents of the University of California, 7 Mar. 2011. Web. 22 July 2015.

13. Caleb Galoozis. "It's the Economy, Stupid." *Harvard University Institute of Politics.* President and Fellows of Harvard College, 2015. Web. 22 July 2015.

CHAPTER 5. GEORGE W. BUSH

1. "George H. W. Bush: Life before the Presidency." *Miller Center.* Rector and Visitors of University of Virginia, n.d. Web. 22 July 2015.

2. Ibid.

3. Ibid.

4. George Lardner Jr. and Lois Romano. "At Height of Vietnam, Bush Picks Guard." *Washington Post.* Washington Post Company, 28 July 1999. Web. 22 July 2015.

5. Ibid.

6. "George H. W. Bush: Family Life." *Miller Center.* Rector and Visitors of University of Virginia, n.d. Web. 22 July 2015.

7. Nicholas D. Kristof. "A Philosophy with Roots in Conservative Texas Soil." *New York Times.* New York Times Company, 21 May 2000. Web. 22 July 2015.

8. Eric Pooley and S. C. Gwynne. "How George Got His Groove." *CNN.* Cable News Network, 14 June 1999. Web. 22 July 2015.

9. "George H. W. Bush: Life before the Presidency." *Miller Center.* Rector and Visitors of University of Virginia, n.d. Web. 22 July 2015.

10. Ibid.

11. Ibid.

12. George W. Bush. *Decision Points.* New York: Crown, 2010. Print. 35.

CHAPTER 6. RETURN TO THE WHITE HOUSE

1. "George H. W. Bush: Campaigns and Elections." *Miller Center.* Rector and Visitors of University of Virginia, n.d. Web. 22 July 2015.

2. Ibid.

3. Ibid.

4. "What Is the Electoral College." *NARA.* NARA, n.d. Web. 22 July 2015.

5. "George H. W. Bush: Domestic Affairs." *Miller Center.* Rector and Visitors of University of Virginia, n.d. Web. 22 July 2015.

6. Kenneth T. Walsh. "George W. Bush's 'Bullhorn' Moment." *US News.* US News & World Report, 25 Apr. 2013. Web. 22 July 2015.

7. "9/11 Resource Guide." *George W. Bush Presidential Library and Museum.* George W. Bush Presidential Library and Museum, n.d. Web. 22 July 2015.

8. George W. Bush. "Address to the Nation on the Terrorist Attacks." *American Presidency Project.* Gerhard Peters and John T. Woolley, n.d. Web. 22 July 2015.

9. "George H. W. Bush: Foreign Affairs." *Miller Center.* Rector and Visitors of University of Virginia, n.d. Web. 22 July 2015.

10. "Bush Announces Strikes against Taliban." *Washington Post.* Washington Post Company, 7 Oct. 2001. Web. 22 July 2015.

11. "George H. W. Bush: Foreign Affairs." *Miller Center.* Rector and Visitors of University of Virginia, n.d. Web. 22 July 2015.

12. Ibid.

13. "Bush's Final Approval Rating: 22 Percent." *CBS News.* CBS Interactive, 16 Jan. 2009. Web. 22 July 2015.

14. "Bush: 'We Need to Change Our Strategy in Iraq.'" *CNN.* Cable News Network, 11 Jan. 2007. Web. 22 July 2015.

CHAPTER 7. JEB BUSH

1. Michael Kranish. "Jeb Bush Shaped by Troubled Phillips Academy Years." *Boston Globe*. Boston Globe Media, 1 Feb. 2015. Web. 22 Aug. 2015.

2. Ibid.

3. Ibid.

4. Stephen L. Bowen, Tarren Bragdon, Jason A. Fortin, and J. Scott Moody. "Governor Jeb Bush: A Record of Leadership and Policy Accomplishment." *Washington Policy Center*. Maine Heritage Policy Center, 2007. Web. 22 July 2015.

5. Michele Richinick. "Barbara Bush Changes Her Mind about Jeb Presidential Campaign." *MSNBC*. NBC Universal, 18 Mar. 2015. Web. 22 July 2015.

CHAPTER 8. THE FUTURE OF THE BUSH FAMILY

1. Molly Ball. "George P. Bush: A Political Dynasty's Young Hope." *Atlantic*. Atlantic Monthly Group, 10 July 2012. Web. 25 June 2015.

2. Ibid.

3. Matthew Waller. "George P. Bush Swears In as Land Commissioner, Continues Family Legacy." *Abilene Reporter-News*. Journal Media Group, 2 Jan. 2015. Web. 22 July 2015.

4. Molly Ball. "George P. Bush: A Political Dynasty's Young Hope." *Atlantic*. Atlantic Monthly Group, 10 July 2012. Web. 25 June 2015.

Carla Mooney is the author of several books for young readers. She loves learning about people, places, and events in history. A graduate of the University of Pennsylvania, she lives in Pittsburgh, Pennsylvania, with her husband and three children.